EYEWITNESS
Activity

NIGHT SKY DETECTIVE

by Ben Morgan
Consultant Dr Jacqueline Mitton

Penguin Random House

REVISED EDITION
Editor Ishani Nandi
Art Editors Mary Sandberg,
Shreya Sadhan
Senior Editors Carron Brown,
Shatarupa Chaudhuri
DTP Designer Pawan Kumar
Senior DTP Designer Harish Aggarwal
Managing Editors Linda Esposito,
Alka Thakur Hazarika
Managing Art Editors Michael Duffy,
Romi Chakraborty
CTS Manager Balwant Singh
Publisher Andrew Macintyre
Producer, Pre-production Adam Stoneham
Senior Producer Gemma Sharpe
Jacket Editor Claire Gell
Jacket Designers Laura Brim, Dhirendra Singh
Managing Jacket Editor Saloni Singh
Jacket Development Manager Sophia MTT
Associate Publishing Director Liz Wheeler
Publishing Director Jonathan Metcalf
Art Director Phil Ormerod

ORIGINAL EDITION
Produced for Dorling Kindersley Ltd by
Cooling Brown Ltd
Creative Director Arthur Brown
Editor Nikki Sims
Designers Tish Jones, Elly King,
Elaine Hewson, Mick Barratt

For Dorling Kindersley Ltd
Senior Editors Fran Baines, Carey Scott
Senior Art Editor Stefan Podhorodecki
Managing Editor Linda Esposito
Managing Art Editor Jane Thomas
Publishing Managers Caroline Buckingham,
Andrew Macintyre
Photography Dave King

First published in Great Britain in 2006
This edition first published in Great Britain
in 2015 by
Dorling Kindersley Limited, 80 Strand,
London WC2R ORL

A CIP catalogue record for this book is available
from the British Library.
ISBN 978-0-2411-8541-4

Colour reproduction by Alta Image Ltd, London, UK
Printed in China

A WORLD OF IDEAS:
SEE ALL THERE IS TO KNOW

Contents

Stargazing

Have you ever looked at the night sky and been amazed by all the stars? If so, this book is for you. Stargazing is the world's oldest hobby, and anyone can try it. It's not just about learning constellations: you can see galaxies and shooting stars, find planets in the night sky, and watch an eclipse.

Where and when

The best time to stargaze is on a dark, clear night when there's no Moon. Winter nights are longer than those in the summer, but you can stargaze all year round. What's more, you'll see different things at different times of the year. You'll see more if you travel out of town, as city lights create a hazy glow called "light pollution", which blocks out all but the brightest stars. If you stargaze from home, turn out the lights in your house and stand in the darkest spot in the garden. Better still, visit the countryside or go on a camping holiday.

Night vision

It takes about 20 minutes for your eyes to adjust to darkness. So, if you're patient and stay in the dark, you'll see more and more stars. Don't look at bright light when your eyes have adjusted, because you'll spoil your night vision. Some people use a red torch for reading star charts and books because red light doesn't interfere with your night vision. Another technique is to close one eye when you're using a torch, so the other remains as sensitive as possible.

A planisphere (star chart) shows which stars are visible at different times and dates

USING THE INTERNET

The Internet is another exciting way to look at space. You can use it to see pictures taken by the world's best telescopes, or by spacecraft and rovers that are exploring the planets. Online planetarium websites can show you exactly which stars and planets are visible from where you live at any time. Astronomy news websites will give you information on forthcoming events to watch out for, such as meteor showers, eclipses, or passing comets.

A Glowing Po... ✕

http://www.spacetelescope.org/images/opo9839a/

Planetary nebula ▲
The latest pictures from the Hubble Space Telescope can be seen on the Internet. This one shows the glowing shell of gas around a dying star.

Useful gear

The only essential equipment for stargazing is warm clothing, as stargazers spend a lot of time standing or sitting still. A star chart (see pages 46–47) or astronomy book is useful if you want to find particular stars. To read them, you'll need a torch. A red torch is best, as it will not affect your night vision. To make one, cover the end with a sheet of clear red plastic film. A compass, a watch, a notepad, and pen are also useful. Binoculars will help you to see small or faint objects much more clearly. Only expensive telescopes are significantly better than binoculars.

A sleeping bag will keep you warm

Keep books and papers off the ground, which may become wet with dew

HANDY TIP

A deckchair makes it much easier to look at the stars without having to lie on the ground.

The sky at night

The night sky can be very bewildering. There are thousands of stars, apparently sprinkled at random. To make matters worse, they are constantly moving around the sky. To help us make sense of the stars, we group them in patterns called constellations. To help us make sense of their movement, we imagine them being fixed to a giant moving globe that surrounds Earth.

The Plough

URSA MAJOR

Constellations

Since the earliest times, people have looked for patterns in the stars to help them remember which star is which. Many constellations were later given names from Roman and Greek myths, such as Orion (the Hunter) and Aries (the Ram). There are 88 internationally recognized constellations, all with Latin names. The Great Bear, for instance, is officially Ursa Major. Some well-known groups of stars are not constellations. The Plough, for example, is part of the Great Bear.

Gamma Cassiopeiae is 615 light-years away from Earth

South celestial pole

Epsilon Cassiopeiae is 440 light-years away from Earth

Alpha Cassiopeiae is 230 light-years away

Beta Cassiopeiae is 54 light-years away

Just an illusion

Constellations are just the patterns we see from Earth. Because the stars that lie in the same direction appear to be in a group, but in reality they can be very far apart. Astronomers measure distances in space in light-years – 1 light-year is the distance that light travels in 1 year (see page 9). The five stars making the "W" in Cassiopeia vary in distance from 54 light-years away to 615 light-years away.

Delta Cassiopeiae is 100 light-years away

CASSIOPEIA

North celestial pole

North Pole

Earth

Ecliptic

South Pole

Celestial equator

The celestial sphere

Stars move across the sky during the night much as the Sun does during the day. They move as though they were fixed points on a gigantic, rotating ball that surrounds Earth. This ball doesn't really exist, but astronomers find it a useful concept and call it the "celestial sphere". The points of the sphere directly over Earth's North and South Poles, where the stars hardly move, are called celestial poles. Halfway between them is the "celestial equator". Every star has a fixed position on the celestial sphere and never shifts from that spot. In contrast, planets move against the starry background.

The yellow line – the ecliptic – is the Sun's apparent path across the celestial sphere

The orange line is the celestial equator. Stars here are visible in both the Northern and the Southern Hemispheres

MEASURING DISTANCE

Astronomers measure distances across the celestial sphere in degrees (°). The whole sphere covers 360°, but at night you can see only half the sphere (180°). You don't have to be a professional astronomer to measure distances; you can use your hand. Hold your hand at arm's length and use the guides shown on the right; these work no matter what age you are.

A finger's width
One finger is about 1° (twice the width of a Full Moon).

Half handspan
A closed hand at arm's length is about 10° across.

Whole handspan
An open hand with fingers fully splayed is about 22°.

Our place in space

For centuries, people thought that planet Earth was the centre of the universe, with all the planets and stars revolving around it. With the invention of the telescope, astronomers started to realize that things were, in fact, quite different. Earth, as it turned out, is a small and insignificant planet orbiting just one of countless quadrillions of stars scattered across the vast cosmos.

Warmth from the Sun causes activity in the atmosphere, which affects the climate on Earth

Planet Earth and its star

Our planet is the only place in the universe known to support life. Earth is just the right distance from the Sun for water to be able to exist in all its forms: liquid water, solid ice, and water vapour. Water is essential for life. It covers two-thirds of the surface of Earth, and fills the sky with clouds. Our Sun is an average star. Its source of power is buried deep in the central core, where nuclear fusion reactions transform matter into energy. The Sun contains nearly all the matter in the solar system. It has tremendously powerful gravity, which keeps the planets trapped in orbit around it.

The planets

The Sun and planets make up the family of bodies that we call the solar system. There are at least eight planets orbiting the Sun, many with their own moons. The inner planets, including Earth, are made of rock and metal. Most of the outer planets are giant globes of hydrogen and helium, left over from the formation of the Sun. Beyond the gas giants lies the tiny, icy dwarf planet Pluto. Between the outer and inner planets is a ring of rocky space debris, called the asteroid belt.

EXPLORING THE COSMOS

Distances in space are too big for the human mind to imagine. Astronomers measure them in light-years – 1 light-year is the distance that light (the fastest thing in the universe) travels in one year, or 10 million million km (6 million million miles). The light we see from stars left them many years ago, and so we are looking back in time. With the world's most powerful telescopes, astronomers can see almost 14 billion light-years across space.

Scanning the skies ▲
An amateur astronomer tries out the telescope at Kitt Peak Observatory, USA. The observatory's domed roof opens to reveal the Milky Way.

The universe

Beyond the planets lies interstellar space, the darkness between the stars. If you travelled for long enough – about 500 years at the speed of a space shuttle – you would reach the Sun's nearest neighbouring star, called Proxima Centauri. It is one of about 200 billion stars that make up our local galaxy, the Milky Way. Every star that you can see in the night sky belongs to this galaxy. Beyond the Milky Way are mind-bogglingly vast stretches of emptiness, and beyond these are yet more galaxies. There are probably hundreds of billions of galaxies stretching into the distance in all directions, but we will never know the exact number because we can see only a fraction of them. The galaxies and all the emptiness of space make up the universe.

Paper planets

Our solar system is made up of the Sun, eight planets, and at least 146 moons. Earth is one of the smaller planets, as you can see for yourself by making this mobile, which shows the planets' relative sizes. This mobile, however, doesn't include the Sun, which at this scale would be twice the height of your room!

WHAT YOU WILL NEED

- Pencil and compasses
- Drawing pin and string
- Cotton
- 18 pieces of card (ideally of eight colours)
- Ruler
- Scissors
- Pole 1.5 m (5 ft)

Planet	Diameter
Mercury	1.5 cm ($\frac{1}{2}$ in)
Venus	4 cm ($1\frac{1}{2}$ in)
Earth	4 cm ($1\frac{1}{2}$ in)
Mars	2 cm ($\frac{3}{4}$ in)
Jupiter	47 cm ($18\frac{1}{2}$ in)
Saturn	39 cm ($15\frac{1}{4}$ in)
Uranus	16 cm ($6\frac{1}{4}$ in)
Neptune	15 cm (6 in)

Tie a pen to some string and mark half the diameter on it. Put a pin on the mark and place it in the centre of the card

1 **Use the pencil** and compasses to draw circles on card for the planets, following the measurements in the table. For the larger circles you will have to use a drawing pin and some string. Draw two circles for each planet.

2 **On each circle**, use the ruler to draw a straight line from the edge to the middle. Then, cut along the length of that line (see picture below). Slot each pair of circles together.

Neptune

3 **Make a pin hole** at the top of each planet and thread some cotton through. Loop the cotton over the pole and tie on each planet in the order in the table. This mobile shows the order and the relative sizes of the planets but doesn't reveal how far apart they are. To make such a scale model, you would need a pole about 20 km (12 miles) long!

Jupiter

Saturn

Uranus

Planetary profiles

There are two kinds of planet. The four inner planets are rock and metal, and the four outer giants are mostly liquid and gas.

Mercury ▶

A heavily cratered ball of rock and iron, Mercury scorches during the day but is freezing at night.

◀ Venus

Though similar in size and structure to Earth, Venus is baking hot and has poisonous acidic air.

Earth ▶

Our home planet is the only place in the solar system known to have liquid water and life.

◀ Mars

Now a freezing, rust-covered desert, Mars had liquid water in the past.

Jupiter ▶

By far the most massive planet, mighty Jupiter has no solid surface and more than 67 moons.

◀ Saturn

Saturn is a "lightweight" version of Jupiter, but with magnificent rings and blurry bands.

Uranus ▶

This blue-green giant has hazy clouds that are hard to see. Oddly, Uranus spins on its side.

◀ Neptune

Violent winds and gigantic storms whip across this giant's deep blue face.

BIRTH OF THE SOLAR SYSTEM

Our solar system formed 5 billion years ago in a vast, interstellar cloud of gas and dust. Part of the cloud began to shrink under its own gravity, and as it contracted it grew hotter and denser, and formed a spinning disc. The disc's core grew so dense and hot that it started shining, forming the Sun. Leftover debris clumped together to form planets and moons.

Formation of a planetary system around a star

Round and round

The planets travel around the Sun along paths called orbits. Their paths are not perfect circles but slightly squashed circles, called ellipses. The planets of the solar system have orbits that are only slightly elliptical, but the dwarf planet Pluto is so elliptical that its orbit overlaps that of Neptune's. You can see how this happens by using loops of string to draw ellipses on a sheet of paper.

WHAT YOU WILL NEED

- Large sheet of paper (A3-sized or bigger)
- Large board that you can push tacks or small nails into
- Coloured pins or tacks
- Ruler
- String
- Pens (one red, one blue)
- Scissors

AROUND THE SUN

Large space bodies orbit the Sun because they are trying to move through space but are trapped by the powerful pull of the Sun's gravity. If you could turn the gravity off, the planets would speed away into space, travelling in straight lines. You can see how this works by tying a weight, such as a washer, to a string and swinging it round and round. The tight string is like the Sun's gravity. The weight would fly off if you let go of the string. If you stop whirling fast enough, the weight falls down. It is only because a planet is moving that it doesn't fall straight into the Sun.

Orbiting worlds ▲
Most of the planets orbit the Sun in roughly the same plane. However, the orbit of the dwarf planet Pluto (the furthest orbit at the back of the picture above) is tilted by about 10° from the rest.

Pluto's orbit is larger and more elliptical than Neptune's

Pluto's orbit

1 **Push two pins** into a large sheet of paper on an old table or a large board. Push the first pin into the middle of the paper – this pin represents the Sun. Push in the second pin exactly 8 cm (3 1/4 in) to the left of the first – this pin helps you draw the ellipse of Pluto's orbit.

2 **Now tie two loops** of string. The first loop should measure 14 cm (5 1/2 in) long when pulled straight. Tie the knot loosely at first, then hold the loop against the ruler and make small adjustments to the knot until the loop is exactly the right length; then, pull tight. Repeat for the second loop but make this one 19 cm (7 1/2 in) long when pulled straight.

TRAPPED IN ORBIT

Satellites monitor the weather, transmit phone and TV signals, and take photographs of places and even people. The speed that a satellite travels depends on how close it is to Earth – the closer the satellite is, the faster it must fly to overcome Earth's gravity. A satellite in orbit 35,790 km (22,240 miles) above Earth takes 24 hours to circle the planet. Earth spins on its axis every 24 hours, so the satellite and planet move together and the satellite stays over the same spot.

A communications satellite

Pluto's orbit passes nearer to the Sun at this point

Neptune's orbit

Reposition the pin to draw Neptune's orbit

Draw Pluto's orbit with the left pin here

Sun

HANDY TIP

Keep the pull on the string firm and even for the smoothest orbit paths.

3 **Place the longest loop** around the pins and hold a blue pen in the loop, pulling the string tight. Carefully draw around the pins, pulling on the string all the time and making sure it doesn't slip off. Label the blue ellipse: Pluto's orbit.

4 **Now reposition** the left pin so that it's only 1 cm ($1/2$ in) to the left of the other pin. Put the shorter loop around the tacks and use the red pen to draw another ellipse. Label this orbit: Neptune's orbit. Although Pluto orbits the Sun farther out than Neptune, you can see that its very elliptical orbit sometimes crosses Neptune's path and so passes closer to the Sun.

Seeing sunspots

The Sun is incredibly bright and you should never look at it directly. But, you can create a safe image of it with binoculars and a screen made from card. You can use this technique to watch planets pass in front of the Sun (transits), to see partial or total solar eclipses (see pages 18–19), and to search for sunspots.

Anchor the binoculars and card securely with books

WHAT YOU WILL NEED

- 2 large pieces of card
- Binoculars
- Scissors
- Paper
- Tape
- Pencil or pen

Don't look directly at the Sun and NEVER look at it through a telescope, binoculars, or even via a mirror.

WHAT ARE SUNSPOTS?

Sunspots are slightly darker, cooler patches on the Sun's surface. They might look small on the image made by your binoculars, but they are big enough to swallow Earth. By tracking sunspots over a period of time, astronomers discovered that the Sun doesn't rotate as a solid object. The poles take 35 days to rotate once, but the equator takes only 25 days.

Sunspots on the Sun's surface

GREAT BALL OF FIRE?

The Sun isn't really a ball of fire but a gigantic globe of superhot hydrogen gas. Its power comes from its sheer weight. It contains 99.9 per cent of all the matter in the solar system, and this huge mass crushes the core and forces atoms together in nuclear fusion reactions. The energy escapes as heat, light, radiation, and violent eruptions from the surface.

Sun storm ▶
A loop of superhot gas erupts from the Sun. Storms like this are most frequent during a "solar maximum" – a period every 11 years when sunspot numbers reach a peak.

_____ *Sun's rays*

1 **Make a shield** to hold the binoculars using some card and scissors. To allow sunlight through one lens only, cover the other lens with card or a lens cap. Prop the shield with the binoculars on a chair so they face the Sun directly, and secure them.

2 **Place the other piece** of card in the shadow of the binoculars, about 1 m (3 ft) away, to act as a screen. Tilt the binoculars until an image of the Sun appears on the screen. Sharpen the image by focusing the binoculars.

3 **Look for dark sunspots** in the image. Tape some paper on to the screen and trace the Sun and any sunspots. Repeat the next day and look for the same sunspots – they will have shifted as the Sun turns.

_____ *Angle the screen so that it's facing the binoculars*

What's the time?

Earth turns around once every 24 hours, and this is why the Sun appears to cross the sky and vanish over the horizon, creating our day and night. Earth's rotation is so regular that you can use the Sun to tell the time. The best way to do this is to build a sundial, a device that was first used around 6,000 years ago.

WHAT YOU WILL NEED

- Pencil
- Block of wood
- Ruler
- Protractor
- Permanent marker pen
- Atlas
- Small piece of thin wood
- Plasticine/modelling clay
- Craft glue
- Compass

Ask an adult to help to construct the solid base.

Use a compass to ensure your sundial faces in the right direction

Solid wooden base

Setting up your sundial

Take the sundial outside and place it on a flat surface. Point the pencil north if you live in the Northern Hemisphere or south if you live in the Southern Hemisphere. If your country adjusts clocks according to the season, the time may be an hour or more out.

2 pm

1 pm

Hour markers

1 **Draw a straight line** across the board 2.5–5 cm (1–2 in) from one end and mark its centre with a dot. Use the protractor to draw rays 15° apart from this point; draw these rays in pencil first in case you make any mistakes. When you've finished, use the permanent marker pen to draw over the pencil lines and write the times as shown (above right). If your base is circular, start from the centre of the board and draw rays all around, as on a clock face.

15°

EARLY TIMEKEEPERS

About 6,000 years ago, people in the Middle East began using shadows to tell the time, and so invented sundials – the world's first clocks. Sundials were popular for centuries, but since they work only when it's sunny, inventors came up with other clock ideas, including notched candles and pendulums. It was only about 150 years ago that mechanical clocks became watch-sized.

Wooden sundial ▶
Some sundials had a compass built into their design for quick and easy telling of the time.

Built-in compass

In the Northern Hemisphere, this end of the pencil should point north – and in the Southern Hemisphere, it should point south

Angle here must match your latitude

6 pm

4 pm

3 pm

9 am

8 am

7 am

6 am

12 noon

11 am

10 am

9 am

— Atlas

HANDY TIP

To weatherproof your sundial, ask an adult to paint it with clear wood varnish.

2 **The part of the sundial** that casts a shadow is called the "gnomon". The angle under the gnomon must be the same as your latitude (see pages 56–57 for more about latitude). Use an atlas to find out your latitude. Then, ask an adult to cut the small piece of wood into a triangle, with one corner cut to the angle of your latitude.

3 **Use the Plasticine** or modelling clay to fix the pencil to the dot in the middle of the line at the end of the board. Position the triangle under the pencil, making sure that the corner matching your latitude is in the Plasticine. Adjust until it all fits snugly, then glue the triangle in place and let the glue set.

When darkness comes

One of the most amazing astronomical events you can ever see is a total solar eclipse, when the Moon passes in front of the Sun. During a total eclipse, the Sun is blocked by the Moon and twilight falls on Earth. During a partial eclipse, the Moon just takes a "bite" out of the Sun.

Diamond ring
Just before and after the Moon covers the Sun during a total solar eclipse, the rays of sunlight may shine through valleys on the Moon, creating a "diamond ring" effect.

How it works
A solar eclipse occurs when the Moon comes directly between the Sun and Earth, blocking out the sunlight and casting a shadow on Earth. The shadow has two parts: the umbra and the penumbra. The umbra is the darkest part of the shadow, where all sunlight is blocked; this is where total eclipses occur. In the penumbra, the Sun is only partly blocked; this is where partial eclipses occur. Partial eclipses are much more common than total eclipses, but less spectacular.

Moon

The inner, darker part of the Moon's shadow (the umbra)

Watch an eclipse safely
Never look directly at the Sun without eye protection officially approved as safe. Sunglasses or home-made filters do not protect your eyes enough. During a total eclipse, it is safe to remove goggles briefly during totality, when the Sun is completely blocked. Do not try to view a partial eclipse, the partial stage of a total eclipse, or the diamond-ring stage with the naked eye.

Stages of an eclipse
The Moon takes about an hour to slide over the Sun in the first stage of a total eclipse. The period when the Sun is completely blocked is called totality and lasts up to 7.5 minutes. During totality, you can see the Sun's delicate outer atmosphere – or corona – stretching out into space.

The early stages of a total eclipse

A total eclipse occurs only in the central part of the Moon's shadow

IMPORTANT

Don't look directly at the Sun and NEVER look at it through a telescope, binoculars, or via a mirror.

The outer part of the Moon's shadow (the penumbra) covers a much wider area

Earth

WATCHING A PARTIAL ECLIPSE

The best way to see a partial eclipse is to make a device called a pinhole camera, which creates an image of the Sun. Cut a small circular hole in one end of a shoe box and tape some kitchen foil over the hole. Then, use compasses to make a pin hole in the foil. At the other end of the box, cut out a square and tape tracing paper over the square to make a screen. During the eclipse, point the pinhole-end of the box towards the Sun, and watch the image appear safely on the paper screen.

Hold the box towards the Sun

Watch the screen

Light enters via the pin hole at one end of the box

Totality

The later stages of a total eclipse

Lunar landscape

The Moon is the closest heavenly body to Earth and the easiest to see. Even with the naked eye you can see the dark lunar "seas" and brighter highlands, but with binoculars or a telescope you can also see a wealth of craters, mountains, and other features.

SCARFACE

The Moon's highlands are covered with craters made by meteorite collisions, but the darker "seas" have few craters. Astronomers think most of the craters formed early in the Moon's history. Earth was battered by meteorites at the same time, but our craters have since been worn away by weather and geological forces. After the bombardment ended, molten lava oozed from the Moon's interior and spread across the lowlands, wiping out some craters and forming the lunar seas, or maria.

A large lunar crater with central hills

The mountains around Mare Imbrium and Serenitatis are the remains of vast crater rims

Oceanus Procellarum (Oceans of Storms)

Mare Humorum (Sea of Moisture)

The Oceans of Storms is the largest of the Moon's maria

Lunar seas are large, level basalt plains on the Moon's surface

When to observe the Moon

The Full Moon is not the best time to view the Moon. All other times are better because the Sun's sideways illumination casts shadows from lunar mountains and crater rims, making them stand out more. The Moon's features are most clear at the "terminator" – the border between the lit and the unlit area. The terminator sweeps across the Moon over the course of a month (see pages 22–23), making different features stand out at different times.

MAKING CRATERS

The Moon has been pounded by so many meteorites that many of the craters overlap or formed on top of older craters. You can create a similar effect with a tray of sand and "meteorites" of varying sizes, such as balls and marbles. Flatten the sand, then drop the meteorites from overhead.

Home-made craters

Plato crater

Mare Imbrium (Sea of Rains)

Mare Serenitatis (Sea of Serenity)

Mare Crisium (Sea of Crises)

Copernicus crater

Mare Tranquillitatis (Sea of Tranquillity)

Mare Fecunditatis (Sea of Fertility)

Theophilus crater ▶

Mare Nectaris (Sea of Nectar)

Apollo 11 landing site where people first stood on the Moon

Mare Nubium (Sea of Clouds)

Tycho crater

The bright rays around Tycho are vast streaks of debris thrown out by the meteorite impact that formed the crater. These are best seen at Full Moon

A lunar calendar

Unlike the Sun, the Moon doesn't make light of its own. Instead we see the Moon in the sky only when it reflects light from the Sun – it acts like an enormous mirror. As the Moon travels around Earth on its monthly orbit, we see it at different angles relative to the Sun. It changes from a thin crescent to a full disc, passing through a series of stages called phases. If you watch the Moon every day for a month, you can record the whole cycle of phases.

WHAT YOU WILL NEED

- Pen
- Sheet of white paper
- Compasses
- Sheet of black paper
- Scissors
- Glue
- Aluminium foil
- Binoculars

1 **Draw a chart** with 29 squares, made of four rows of seven squares and one extra square (see right). Cut out 29 circles from the black paper and stick one in each square.

Write the numbers 1 to 29 in the squares

2 **Wait for a clear night** when you can see the Moon. Look at the Moon's shape (binoculars might help, but they aren't essential). Cut out its shape to match in aluminium foil and glue it on to the first black circle of the chart.

3 **Do the same** every day for a month. To find out when the Moon rises and sets each day, look in a newspaper. Some nights will be cloudy, so leave those blank.

THE PHASES OF THE MOON

At New Moon, the Moon is between Earth and the Sun. It crosses the sky during daylight hours, but we don't see it because it's hidden by the Sun's glare, and only its far side is sunlit. Over the next days, the Moon moves away from the Sun in the sky and sunlight spills around its edge, forming a crescent that is easiest to see after sunset. When half the Moon's face is lit, it is a quarter of the way through its orbit (first quarter), and at this stage is visible from noon to midnight. As the sunlit area grows (waxes), we see the Moon more at night. When it is halfway through its orbit, it is opposite the Sun and fully lit in the night sky – then, we see it as a Full Moon.

Full Moon

Waning Gibbous

Waxing Gibbous

Last Quarter

The changing face of the Moon

First Quarter

Waning Crescent

Waxing Crescent

New Moon (not visible from Earth)

Moon detective

If you have binoculars, take a close look at the Moon each day. You'll see different features as the month progresses, and the angle of sunlight striking the Moon changes. The best place to look is near the terminator – the dividing line between the areas of shadow and light.

Aluminium foil

Moon shadows

A lunar eclipse takes place when the Moon passes through Earth's shadow. This happens maybe once or twice a year, but it's always worth watching because each eclipse is different. Lunar eclipses are also safe to watch and easy to see – you can watch one from anywhere with a view of the Moon.

Moon in penumbra

Penumbra

Umbra

Sunlight travels from the Sun towards Earth

Earth blocks the light and casts a shadow

An eclipse happens when the Moon enters the umbra

How it works ▲

Lunar eclipses can happen only at Full Moon, when the Moon is on the opposite side of Earth from the Sun and comes close to Earth's shadow. Earth's shadow has two parts: an outer zone called the penumbra, where sunlight is reduced; and an inner zone called the umbra, where all direct sunlight is blocked. A total eclipse is when the whole Moon enters the umbra. If only part of the Moon enters the umbra, it is a partial eclipse.

◄ Viewing an eclipse

You don't need special equipment to watch an eclipse, but binoculars or a good-quality telescope allow you to see extra details. Total lunar eclipses are the most interesting but they don't happen every year. To find out when the next one is due and where you can see it, look up lunar eclipses on the Internet.

Moon entering umbra

Moon approaching totality

Stages of an eclipse

The main eclipse begins when the Moon first enters the umbra. A dark shadow appears on the side of the Moon and slowly creeps across it over the next hour or so. At the same time, moonlight fades and the sky darkens. The Moon looks different from a normal crescent at this stage because the shadow is much less curved and lacks a crisp edge. When the shadow covers the Moon entirely, the Moon is totally eclipsed but still faintly visible. Totality lasts anything up to 1 hour 47 minutes. Afterwards, the earlier stages of the eclipse are repeated, but in reverse.

WHY DOESN'T THE MOON DISAPPEAR?

Try this activity to find out why the Moon doesn't disappear completely during an eclipse. Line up a ball, a globe, and a desk lamp in a dark room. Imagine that the globe is Earth and the ball is the Moon. Switch on the light and place the ball in Earth's shadow. Now, mix an "atmosphere" for Earth: add a teaspoon of milk to a clear plastic bottle and fill with water. Hold the bottle on top of the globe and watch the Moon. The milky water scatters light, casting a pinkish glow on the Moon even though it's in Earth's shadow.

The ball represents the Moon

The milky water represents Earth's atmosphere

The globe blocks the light, casting a shadow

Desk lamp

Totality

The most spectacular part of a lunar eclipse is totality, when the Moon is completely within the umbra. Sunlight scattered by Earth's atmosphere can turn the Moon copper red during totality. It's also the time when stars are brightest and the Milky Way may become more visible.

Escape velocity

The faster an object moves, the harder it is to stop. This principle governs the movement of planets, moons, stars, and spacecraft, which hurtle through space at terrific speed but are pulled towards each other by gravity. With bearings and a magnet, you can investigate how speed (velocity) can help objects escape the forces pulling them.

WHAT YOU WILL NEED

- Scissors
- An old cereal box
- Book
- Plasticine/modelling clay
- Flat magnet
- Steel ball bearings
- Large magnet

1 **Cut a strip of card** 30 cm long by 6 cm wide (12 in by 3 in) from a cereal box and fold it into a "V" shape.

2 **Raise one end** on a book and fix it to a piece of Plasticine or modelling clay to form a long ramp. Place a flat magnet under the other end of the ramp.

3 **Roll steel bearings** down the ramp. Start from a low position on the ramp and see if they roll past the magnet or stick to it. Then try higher positions and see if they roll over the magnet without sticking. Adjust the steepness of the ramp if they always stick or never stick.

The speed of the bearing determines whether or not it sticks to the magnet or escapes its magnetic field

THE PULL OF GRAVITY

Gravity is an invisible force that pulls all objects in the universe together. Massive objects, such as planets, have powerful gravity. Their gravity works like the magnet in this experiment, capturing objects that fly past. Slow-moving objects are pulled in so powerfully that they crash into the surface, or end up trapped in orbit as moons. Fast-moving objects hurtle past and are not trapped, although the force of gravity might deflect their path, or even speed them up.

◄ Deep impact
A massive asteroid succumbs to gravity and crashes into Earth in this artist's impression. A collision like this may have wiped out the dinosaurs.

Adjust the angle of the ramp to control the speed of the bearings

HANDY TIP

Turn the magnet lengthways if the bearings roll past too easily.

Upturned fridge magnet

4 **Remove the flat magnet** and see where a bearing will roll without anything in its way. Then place a powerful magnet near the end of the ramp, but to one side. Try again and see how the magnetic force bends the bearing's path. You may need to keep adjusting the magnet's position until it has a noticeable effect without trapping the bearing.

Use a powerful magnet to deflect the path of the bearings

Up, up, and away!

Just as the bearings in this experiment had to reach a certain speed to escape the magnet, spacecraft must reach a certain speed – called escape velocity – to escape the pull of Earth's gravity. Escape velocity at Earth's surface is 40,000 kph (25,000 mph). Anything travelling upwards at a slower speed than this will fall back down. It takes powerful rockets to accelerate spacecraft to reach escape velocity. But most rockets usually aim only to reach orbital velocity – the speed at which satellites and other cargo become trapped in orbit around Earth.

Ariane 5 ▶
The European rocket Ariane 5 is equipped with two side boosters and two main rocket stages. All are needed to carry space probes fast enough to escape Earth's pull.

Ready for lift-off

Rockets are launched into space by the hot gases from the burning fuel rushing backwards out of their engines. A balloon will fly through the air in just the same way if you let the gas inside it escape. If you use two balloons, as shown here, you can make a simple model of a two-stage rocket.

ROCKET STAGES

When ready for lift-off, a rocket can weigh thousands of tonnes, and almost all of that is due to the fuel on board. It takes immense power to lift such a huge weight off the ground and propel it all the way up into space. To make the job easier, rockets are divided into a series of two or three stages, stacked on top of each other. When each stage has used up its fuel, it falls away to lighten the load, making the job of the next stage easier. Only the tip of the rocket makes it all the way into space.

◄ **Separation**
When each stage is spent, explosive charges separate it from the rocket. This explosion prompts boosters to ignite in the next stage.

Point the rocket upwards before you launch it

If you need help, ask an adult to cut the bottom off the cup

1 **Carefully cut** the bottom out of a large plastic or paper cup. Partially inflate a long balloon and pull the open end through the bottom of the cup.

Use the longest balloon you can get

2 **Blow more air** into the long balloon but don't fully inflate it. Fold the end over the bottom of the cup and tape it in place.

ROCKETS OF THE FUTURE

Rockets carry two fuels: liquid hydrogen and liquid oxygen. Hundreds of tonnes of both are needed, which not only makes rockets heavy but also makes launches incredibly expensive. To cut costs, engineers are designing rockets that work like jet engines, sucking in oxygen from the air rather than carrying it on board. Such "air-breathing" craft would be lighter and more manoeuvrable than current rockets or space shuttles. They might even carry tourists on day trips to space.

▲ **Space express**
This artist's impression shows one design for an air-breathing rocket to replace the space shuttle.

HANDY TIP

Tape a straw to the long balloon and guide the rocket along some nylon line.

The long balloon forms the second stage of this rocket

The small, first-stage balloon keeps the end of the long balloon closed

Temporarily tape the end of the long balloon

3 **Push the round balloon** in the bottom of the cup and inflate it so it holds the first balloon closed. Remove the tape holding the long balloon. Now, release the balloon and see how far the rocket travels.

Finding Venus

The lone bright star that often appears in the evening as the Sun goes down is not a star at all, but the planet Venus. Venus is the nearest planet to Earth, and the brightest object in the night sky after the Moon. Sunlight reflected from its dense clouds can make Venus 15 times brighter than the brightest star.

EARTH'S UGLY SISTER

Of all the planets, Venus is most like Earth. It's about the same size, has a similar composition, and has a cloudy atmosphere. But, unlike Earth, Venus is a roasting, waterless desert, far too hot for life – the surface temperature is 482°C (900°F). One reason for the extreme heat on Venus is that it's nearer to the Sun. Another reason is that its dense atmosphere is full of carbon dioxide gas, which traps heat by the "greenhouse effect".

◄ **Through the clouds**
Clouds cover Venus, but radar cameras can see through. This image reveals volcanoes, twisting valleys, and ancient lava flows.

1 **Go outside** on a clear evening just after sunset and look west, towards the sunset. Alternatively, go out just before dawn and look east. If you can see a single, very bright "star" that doesn't twinkle, it's probably Venus. Venus is always close to the Sun, so as the sky darkens and the Sun sinks deeper beyond the horizon, Venus will set too.

Moon

Venus

ON THE SURFACE

Some call Venus the "closest thing to hell in the solar system". The clouds are rich in deadly sulphuric acid, the air is hot enough to melt lead, and the air pressure is 90 times that on Earth. If you landed there, you'd be poisoned, roasted, and crushed to death in seconds. The lethal surface conditions also destroy spacecraft. The *Venera 13* probe holds the record, surviving for 127 minutes.

Venusian mountains ▲
Scientists used radar data to create this 3D view across the highlands of Venus. Some of the mountains might be volcanoes.

2 **Look at Venus** with binoculars. You won't see any surface details because the planet is covered with thick cloud. But, sometimes you can see a crescent shape formed by the pattern of sunlight and shade on the planet (just as the Moon sometimes forms a crescent). Venus looks biggest when it's a crescent, and smallest when it's full, because of the way we see it during its orbit.

Going through phases
Venus' appearance changes as it orbits the Sun. As it approaches its closest point to Earth, we see a large crescent Venus. As it reaches its farthest point from Earth, we see a small disc. Halfway between these points we see a semicircle, and when Venus lines up exactly with the Sun, we don't see it at all because it is lost in the Sun's glare.

Crescent Venus

Sun

Earth

Why is Mars red?

The Greeks named the planet Mars after a god of war because its colour reminded them of blood. The colour is easy to see with the naked eye when Mars passes close to Earth, though it's more of an orangey-brown than a red. The cause, as you can find out for yourself, is a very familiar substance: rust, or iron oxide.

WHAT YOU WILL NEED

- Sand
- Tray
- Rubber gloves
- Scissors
- Wire wool
- Jug of salty water (1 teaspoon of salt to 2 or 3 cupfuls of water)

In 1997, the Sojourner rover landed on Mars and studied chemicals in the rocks

Iron oxide in the dust on Mars gives the planet its colour

SIGNS OF WATER

Three billion years ago, water may have flowed on Mars. The planet probably had shallow oceans, a thick atmosphere, and life. Today, Mars is a bitterly cold desert, with air so thin that liquid water would vaporize in seconds. Space probes have photographed freshly eroded gullies on Mars, in places like Newton Basin. Perhaps such features formed when underground ice reserves thawed and seeped to the surface. Evidence that water still exists was found by the *Curiosity* rover. Liquid water wasn't seen, but in 2013, *Curiosity* detected water vapour in Martian dust.

Newton Basin

1 **Place a layer of sand** on the bottom of a tray. Put the rubber gloves on and use the scissors to snip wire wool into small bits across the sand. Try to pull the bits apart to stop the wire wool clumping and to help spread it out through the sand. While wearing the gloves, mix it well into the sand with your hands.

THE RED PLANET

Scientists are not sure how the iron oxide on Mars formed. On Earth, rust forms when iron reacts with the oxygen in air, a process that is much faster when water is present. But Mars has no liquid water on the surface and its air is almost oxygen-free. Some experts think the iron oxide formed long ago when iron in Martian rocks reacted with water in ancient rivers and seas. Another theory is that the iron built up from tiny meteorites raining on to the surface.

Martian weather ▶
The Hubble Space Telescope took this picture of Mars. It shows an ice cap at its south pole, swirling clouds of ice in the north, and a dust storm in the southeast.

HANDY TIP

Stir the sand around each day to create an even colour.

2 **Pour the salty water** on the sand to wet it but without covering it completely. Leave the tray where it won't be disturbed for a few days.

3 **Check the tray** daily and add water if it dries out. The sand will slowly turn rusty red – like Martian soil.

Is there life on Mars?

In 1976, scientists sent two spacecraft – the *Viking* landers – to Mars to test the dusty soil for signs of microscopic organisms. This activity mimics one of the tests, using sand instead of Martian soil. First, you add nutrients to the sand, then you wait for a reaction. Chemicals in the sand may react quickly but briefly. Living cells (such as yeast) will react slowly but increasingly as they feed and multiply.

WHAT YOU WILL NEED

- Three jars
- Clean, dry sand
- Three coloured labels
- Three teaspoons
- Salt
- Baking powder
- Dried yeast
- Warm water
- Caster sugar
- Glass jug
- Vinegar

HANDY TIP

This experiment can make a mess, so stand your jars on a tray or old newspaper.

Nothing happens in the red jar

1 **Half fill three jars** with dry (or dryish) sand and stick differently coloured labels on them. Using different teaspoons (to prevent contamination), add 2 teaspoons of salt to the red jar, 2 teaspoons of baking powder to the yellow jar, and 2 teaspoons of yeast to the blue jar. Give each jar a stir or shake (with the lid on or a hand over the top) to mix the powder and sand thoroughly.

The sand and salt are thoroughly mixed

Sand with added salt

2 **Pour two cupfuls** of warm water into the glass jug. Add half a cupful of caster sugar and, once dissolved, add 2 teaspoons of vinegar.

3 **Carefully pour** an equal amount of sugar water into each jar. Don't pour it suddenly as it could produce froth and spoil the experiment. Is there an immediate reaction in any of the jars?

SEARCHING FOR SIGNS OF LIFE

The *Viking* landers found no clear evidence of life on Mars, but the hunt goes on. Scientists now know that Mars once had and still has liquid water, a vital ingredient for life. While all tests by spacecraft have been inconclusive to date, the search continues for evidence of past and present life forms.

Spirit rover ▶
In 2004, the *Spirit* rover found evidence that Mars once had water. In 2013, *Curiosity* found water and is now searching for life.

A slow, dramatic reaction happens in the blue jar as yeast cells feed on the sugar and multiply

There is a brief chemical reaction in the yellow jar as the baking powder reacts with the vinegar

Sand with added baking powder

4 **Have a look** after 1 hour, and then again after 2 hours. What kind of reaction would you expect if there were living organisms present?

Sand with added yeast

Stormy weather

Gigantic Jupiter is the largest planet of all – more than twice the weight of all the other planets combined. It is a colossal ball of liquid covered with swirling gases. Its ferocious winds and storms stir the gases into colourful stripes and whirlpools. You can create a very similar effect with milk and food colouring.

WHAT YOU WILL NEED

- Large bowl
- Full-fat milk
- Teaspoon
- Red and yellow food colouring
- Washing-up liquid

Spots and stripes

In Jupiter's freezing upper atmosphere, the gases have condensed into stripy clouds coloured by a cocktail of chemicals. Spots and ovals are storms. Jupiter's Great Red Spot is a hurricane twice the size of Earth that has been raging for 300 years.

HANDY TIP

Rest the bowl on the table as you turn it so that it moves gently and smoothly.

The food colouring floats on the surface of the milk

Great Red Spot

Swirly patterns form as the liquids rotate

1 **Carefully pour** half a mug of full-fat milk into a large mixing bowl. Pour it down the side of the bowl so it doesn't splash and form bubbles on the surface. Let it stand for a minute until the milk is still.

2 **With great care,** use a teaspoon to add a big drop of each food colouring to the surface of the milk. Do this by touching the milk gently with the spoon, and don't stir.

3 **Turn the bowl** around gently so that the milk and food colouring start to swirl, like the coloured clouds in Jupiter's storms. It takes some practice to get a really good storm. Experiment with different amounts of food colouring, and take care not to swirl the bowl too quickly.

Voyager **spacecraft**

Exploring Jupiter

Astronauts could never visit Jupiter because the planet is surrounded by deadly radiation and has no solid surface to land on. But, eight robotic space probes have made trips there. Two *Voyager* spacecraft visited Jupiter in 1979 and sent back more than 33,000 photos as well as a film of clouds swirling around the Great Red Spot.

SUICIDE PROBE

In 1995, a coffee-table-sized package parachuted into Jupiter's clouds to study the planet's stormy weather. The *Galileo* probe hit Jupiter at 185,000 kph (115,000 mph) but soon slowed down in the "thick" air. Its canopy opened, and the probe spent nearly an hour measuring the wind and analysing chemicals before heat destroyed it.

The *Galileo* probe

4 **To kick up** a really violent storm, add a single drop of washing-up liquid. This will disperse the colours quickly by helping the food colouring dissolve.

Jupiter and its moons

Jupiter is one of the brightest planets you can see from Earth. Through good binoculars you can see its rounded shape and its four largest moons. With a telescope, you can even see its stripes.

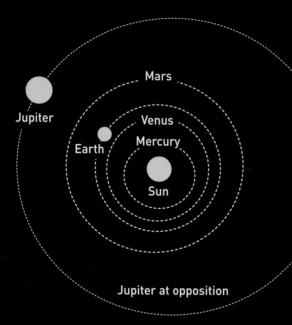

Mars
Jupiter
Venus
Earth
Mercury
Sun
Jupiter at opposition

1 **Find out** when Jupiter is at "opposition" – that is, when Jupiter's orbit brings it closest to Earth and on exactly the opposite side of Earth from the Sun, making Jupiter visible all night. You can see Jupiter easily for weeks before, and after, opposition. In the period after opposition, Jupiter is high in the evening sky, so it's easy to see without staying up late.

Dates when Jupiter is at opposition	Constellation it appears in
8 March 2016	Leo
7 April 2017	Virgo
9 May 2018	Libra
10 June 2019	Ophiuchus
14 July 2020	Sagittarius
20 August 2021	Capricornus
26 September 2022	Pisces
3 November 2023	Aries
7 December 2024	Taurus

Lining up
Sometimes several planets line up – an event known as an "alignment". This picture shows an alignment of Jupiter (left), Mars (middle), and Venus (right). Planets never align perfectly because their orbits don't lie in exactly the same plane.

HANDY TIP
Jupiter and other planets are easy to tell apart from stars because they don't twinkle.

2 **Search for Jupiter** in the month before, or after, opposition. Go out on a clear night and use a compass to face south if you live in the Northern Hemisphere, or north if you live in the Southern Hemisphere. Using a planisphere (see pages 44–45), locate the constellation listed in the table on the left, then look in that constellation for an unusually bright and yellowish "star" that doesn't twinkle – that's Jupiter.

WHAT YOU WILL NEED

- Compass
- Planisphere
- Binoculars

Four of a kind

At least 67 moons orbit Jupiter, trapped in the massive planet's powerful gravity. Many are captured asteroids, but several are so big that we'd call them planets if they orbited the Sun. The four largest are called the Galilean moons, after the Italian astronomer Galileo. Their order from Jupiter is Io, Europa, Ganymede, then Callisto, and the closer they are to Jupiter, the more active they are. Below they are shown in order of size, smallest first.

Europa ▶

Sheets of ice cover this moon, but there may be an ocean of liquid water deep beneath. Some scientists think primitive life forms might live in this hidden ocean.

Io ▶

The most volcanically active object in the solar system, Io has more than 100 volcanoes spewing sulphur and gas far out into space. The volcanic activity leads to changes in Io's surface colour.

Callisto ▶

Billions of years ago, meteorites rained down on this moon and peppered its surface with craters. Since then, Callisto seems to have barely changed. Like Europa, this moon may have a subsurface ocean, but the evidence for this is uncertain.

Ganymede ▶

The largest Galilean moon is Ganymede. This world is a mixture of rock and ice, with white scars where swirling forces inside the moon have cracked the surface. Ganymede has mountains, valleys, and solidified lava flows of ice.

You can see the four largest moons via binoculars as pinpricks of light. Look again on a different night to see how their patterns change

3 **Look at Jupiter** with binoculars. Rest your elbows on a firm surface to steady your view. Can you see Jupiter's four largest moons? If any are missing, they may be in front of, or behind, Jupiter.

Saturn's strange shape

Saturn is nearly ten times wider than Earth, yet it spins more than twice as fast. It rotates so quickly that its equator bulges outwards, making Saturn the flattest planet in our solar system. The force that creates the bulge is called centrifugal force, and you can see it for yourself by making a spinning paper model.

WHAT YOU WILL NEED

- Scissors
- A4 paper in two colours
- Ruler
- Kebab skewer
- Adhesive tape
- Drinking straw
- Long rubber band
- Metal ring (from a keyring or similar)
- Plasticine/modelling clay
- Pencil

In a spin
Saturn rotates once every 10 hours 39 minutes, its equator whizzing around at a dizzying 35,000 kph (22,000 mph). As a result, Saturn is about 10 per cent wider than it is tall.

Centrifugal force pushes the paper strips, making them curve outwards in the middle

Ensure the strips are evenly spaced

1 **Cut the end** off two sheets of A4-sized coloured paper so that they are about 5 cm (2 in) shorter than your skewer. Then cut the paper into long thin strips, each about 0.5 cm (1/4 in) long. Neatly lay about 20 strips, alternating the colours, flat on a table. Place a length of tape across each end of the strips to stick to them all at once (see above). Now lift up the entire sheet, being careful not to lose any of the strips, and flip it over.

2 **Add another two lengths** of tape at the edges only this time, allowing extra at each end. Again, carefully lift and turn the sheet over. Cut two small pieces from the drinking straw and stick one at the end of each length of tape.

Allow enough tape to stick to the straws

Second piece of straw

Strips are neat and flat

LORD OF THE RINGS

Saturn's magnificent rings make this planet one of the wonders of the solar system. They stretch some 480,000 km (300,000 miles) from Saturn's cloud tops, and the faint, outermost ring is farther from Saturn than the Moon is from Earth. Though vast in width, the rings are only tens of metres thick and seem to disappear when seen edge-on. They are made of billions of sparkling fragments of rock and ice, ranging in size from dust particles to enormous boulders kilometres across. The fragments are thought to be debris from a catastrophic collision, perhaps between a moon and a comet.

Rings within rings ▲
Space probes have shown Saturn's rings to be made of thousands of smaller ringlets. The gaps between the rings are cleared by gravity from nearby moons.

HANDY TIP

Roll the two straws slowly over the tape at the same time using equal speed and pressure.

Squeeze firmly to secure everything in place

3 **Pass a kebab skewer** through the straws. Now, carefully roll the tape around the straws, taking care not to let the paper strips get bunched up and stick it down.

4 **Tie a long elastic band** on to the metal ring and attach it to both the skewer and the top of the device with a blob of Plasticine.

5 **Loop the elastic band** over a pencil. Twirl the device round to twist the band, then release to let it spin.

Ensure that the bottom can move freely up and down the skewer

Shooting stars

When specks of rock debris hit Earth's atmosphere and burn up, they make streaks of light called shooting stars. You can see shooting stars every clear night, but they are more common at certain times of year when they fall in "meteor showers". Most shooting stars are caused by debris the size of a grain of sand, but occasional apple-sized rocks produce fantastic fireballs with long tails.

1 **Choose a clear, moonless night** and a dark location far from city lights to see the most shooting stars. It's best to watch after midnight, when Earth's night-side faces incoming space debris head-on, producing faster and brighter shooting stars. You should see a shooting star about every 15 minutes or so.

2 **Take a folding camping chair** and make sure you're comfortable. The two biggest challenges for a shooting-star spotter are cold and patience. To keep you occupied, use a constellation guide and try to identify as many constellations as possible, or watch for shooting stars with a friend or parent. To keep you warm while you're waiting, wear lots of clothes and take a sleeping bag.

SPECTACULAR COMETS

Comets are gigantic balls of ice and dust that occasionally swoop through the inner solar system and become visible from Earth. As a comet approaches the Sun, its icy surface warms up and evaporates, releasing a glowing tail of gas and dust. When Earth passes through the trail of dust left by a comet, the dust particles cause meteor showers.

◄ **A comet's tails**
Comet Hale-Bopp passed Earth in 1997 with a blue and a white tail. The tails of a comet point away from the Sun, whichever way it flies.

WHAT YOU WILL NEED

- Folding chair or recliner
- Photocopy of your star chart to sketch on
- Warm clothes
- Sleeping bag
- Notepad
- Pen

Never go out alone at night – ask an adult to come along too. Dress warmly.

METEOR SHOWERS

A shower of meteors

During a meteor shower you might see dozens of shooting stars an hour. On rare occasions, the rate goes up to thousands an hour – a "meteor storm". Meteor showers happen at the same time each year, when Earth's orbit crosses the dust trail of a comet. The paths of the meteors are in fact parallel, but appear to radiate out from a single point because of their position and distance from Earth.

Warm clothes are essential when you're watching shooting stars, even in summer

HANDY TIP

A fully reclining lounger makes it even more comfortable to skywatch for long periods.

3 **During a meteor shower**, shooting stars all appear to come from the same point in the sky – the radiant. Most meteor showers are named after the constellation in which the radiant is located. Try to work out where the radiant is by sketching each shooting star on a photocopied star chart (see pages 46–47). Make a note of the size and colour of each shooting star.

A star map

One of the most useful bits of kit a stargazer can have is a planisphere. With this simple device, you can find out exactly what stars you're looking at on any night, at any time. You can buy a planisphere at a bookshop, but you can also make one. It has two parts: a base showing a star chart and a rotating mask with an oval window.

WHAT YOU WILL NEED

- Access to a photocopier or colour scanner, computer, and printer
- Glue
- Card
- Scissors
- Atlas
- Sheet of stiff, clear plastic
- Paper fastener
- Compass

Selecting the time and date

The numbers around the edge of the mask show the time of day. Turn the mask around until the time lines up with the date. The window now shows all the visible constellations. Remember that the stars in the sky will appear much smaller and more spread out than on the planisphere.

Mask

Clear plastic

Paper fastener

Star chart

Stiff card

The layers of the planisphere

1 **Photocopy the mask** in colour, if you can, along with the appropriate star chart (see pages 46–47); use an enlargement factor of 200 per cent. Or, scan them on to a computer and print them in colour at double size. Glue the paper to some stiff card and trim the paper and the card with scissors.

Choosing the correct mask
Check your latitude in an atlas and cut out the mask that is nearest.

Selecting the correct time
Use white numbers for the time in the Northern Hemisphere; black numbers for the Southern Hemisphere.

35°
42°
52°

N
W — E
S
Southern Hemisphere

S
E — W
N
Northern Hemisphere

Planisphere mask

Using your planisphere
Once you've lined up the time and date (see left), use a compass to check that north or south is on your right and hold the planisphere above your head. Try to match constellations in the sky to those on the planisphere. It's tricky at first but becomes easier with practice.

2 **Check your latitude** in an atlas and cut out the relevant oval on the mask. Stick your mask to some clear plastic and trim the plastic to match the size of the star chart.

3 **Push a hole** through the middle (carefully using closed scissors) and attach both layers with a paper fastener so that the discs can turn freely.

Star charts

These charts show the brightest stars visible to the naked eye on a clear night. There are two charts: one centred on the north celestial pole, and one on the south celestial pole (there is overlap). You can see only half the sky at any time. To find out which stars are visible on a particular night, use a chart to make a planisphere (see pages 44–45).

Constellations

The labels and yellow lines on the charts show the patterns of stars that astronomers call constellations. On an average night, you'll see only the brightest stars, so don't worry if you find it difficult recognizing many constellations. But, it does get easier with practice.

Northern Hemisphere constellations

READING THE CHARTS

Star charts can be confusing when you start using them. Because they show the whole dome of the night sky in a small area, the stars look much closer together than they really are. The charts also seem to show that some stars are bigger than others, but in fact they are really showing the stars' brightness, or "magnitude". The large dots represent the brightest stars, which are easiest to see. Small dots are faint stars, which are visible only on the darkest, clearest nights. Astronomers use a scale of numbers for magnitude. The scale goes backwards, so large numbers represent faint stars. The naked eye can see stars down to a magnitude of 6. Sirius, the brightest star in the sky, has a magnitude of –1.4, and a Full Moon can reach –13.

▲ Orion with Sirius showing just above the horizon

Southern Hemisphere constellations

Compass stars

Because Earth is spinning, the stars appear to rotate around the night sky. But, there are two points that never move – the north and south celestial poles. These are always at the same points in the sky, due north and due south. Once you know how to find a celestial pole, you can use it as a compass to find your way.

Star trails

If you take a long-exposure photograph of the night sky, the stars' movement across it will create circles of light called "star trails". As well as showing the apparent movement of stars (actually caused by Earth's rotation), star trails reveal the stars' different colours. The central star in this picture is Polaris (the Pole Star), which is about 1° away from the true celestial pole, so it makes a short but bright streak.

FIND THE NORTH CELESTIAL POLE

If you live in the Northern Hemisphere, you can see the north celestial pole, but not the southern one. Finding the north celestial pole is fairly easy because there's a star that almost exactly marks the spot: the Pole Star, Polaris.

1 **To find Polaris**, first locate the Plough – one of the brightest groups of stars to see. It's always visible in the Northern Hemisphere (if you live at latitude 40° or more), though it's much lower in the night sky in autumn than in spring, when it's overhead at midnight.

2 **Draw an imaginary line** from the Plough between the last two stars – the "Pointers" – and extend it five times the distance between the stars to take you to Polaris. Measuring three hand-widths from the Pointers will also take you to Polaris. If you face Polaris (due north), you can work out all directions.

URSA MINOR

Polaris (Pole Star)

The Plough

Pointers

FIND THE SOUTH CELESTIAL POLE

For people who live in the Southern Hemisphere, the south celestial pole is always above the horizon at the same point, due south. However, it's trickier to find than the north celestial pole because there are no stars visible near it – just a blank area of sky.

Southern Cross

Southern Pointers

South celestial pole

1 **First, locate the Southern Cross** – a distinctive constellation in the southern sky. Like the Plough, the Southern Cross is visible throughout the year because it's quite close to the pole. The easiest way to find it is to look for two exceptionally bright stars nearby, called the Southern Pointers, which point to the Southern Cross.

2 **Draw an imaginary line** from the base of the Southern Cross (the star Acrux). Extend it by about five times the "height" of the cross, or three hand-widths, to take you to the south celestial pole. You could also imagine a straight line at right angles to the Pointers. The pole lies where this line intersects the line from the cross.

Northern star-hopping

If you live in the Northern Hemisphere, you can use the Plough and Polaris (the Pole Star) as stepping stones to find other stars. Try finding some of the constellations near Polaris, which are in the sky all year round. You will need a clear, dark night to see them all, as some are faint.

1 **First, find the Plough** and locate the "Pointers" – the last two stars in the Plough. Draw an imaginary line **(a)** from the Pointers and extend it to the Pole Star, Polaris. Polaris is part of the faint constellation Ursa Minor, which you can see only on clear, dark nights.

2 **Extend the line** a little way past Polaris to find the faint constellation Cepheus, which looks like a lopsided house. If you have binoculars, sweep the area around the base of the "house". You'll see a very red star – the Garnet Star. This is the reddest star visible to the naked eye and the largest star yet discovered.

3 **Draw a new line (b)** to Polaris from the third star in the Plough's handle, and then onwards to a bright constellation that looks like a flattened letter W. This is Cassiopeia. You can use the positions of the Plough and Cassiopeia to tell the time (see pages 54–55).

The lozenge

DRACO

URSA MINOR

b

c

URSA MAJOR
(The Plough)

a

M81 galaxy

The Pointers

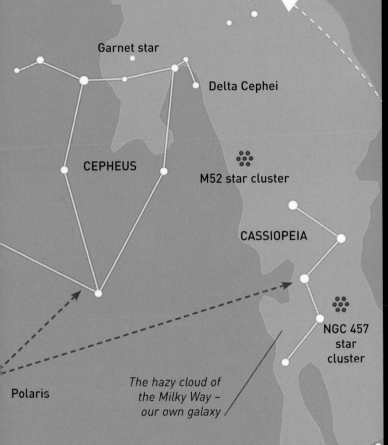

Garnet star

Delta Cephei

CEPHEUS

M52 star cluster

CASSIOPEIA

NGC 457
star
cluster

Polaris

*The hazy cloud of
the Milky Way –
our own galaxy*

Polar constellations

◄ Ursa Minor
Also known as the Little Bear,
this faint constellation looks like
a miniature version of the Plough.
Its brightest star is Polaris, which
has been used for centuries as
an aid to navigation. Sailors used to call Polaris
"Stella Maris", which means "star of the sea".

Ursa Major ►
The seven stars of the
Plough make up the tail
and rump of the Great
Bear, or Ursa Major as
it's officially known. One
of its most interesting
"stars" is the second star along the handle of
the Plough. If you look closely and have sharp
eyes, you will see it's actually a double star.

◄ Cassiopeia
The ancient Greeks named this
constellation after a vain queen, and
pictured her on a throne, admiring
herself in a mirror. Cassiopeia lies in
the band of the Milky Way. Sweep this
area with binoculars to see if you can
see several star clusters around it.

Cepheus ►
In Greek mythology, Cepheus
was married to Cassiopeia.
An interesting star in this
constellation is Delta Cephei,
which is a "variable star".
Variable stars pulse in size and
brightness. Delta Cephei has a
5-day cycle so you can watch it
change with binoculars over
successive nights.

◄ Draco
Draco means "dragon" – an apt
name for a constellation that snakes
across the night sky. The name was
also chosen for Harry Potter's arch
enemy Draco Malfoy. If you've got
some good binoculars and a clear,
dark night, then sweep the area along the dragon's
tail to see if you can find any double stars. Don't
worry if you can't make any out, as many
stars in Draco are quite faint.

4 **The next constellation** is faint
and tricky to see, so look for it
only if the sky is very dark. Draw a line
(c) starting from the fourth star in the
Plough's handle (as shown) to a long,
winding constellation called Draco.
Four stars make up the dragon's head –
a pattern of stars called the "lozenge".

5 **Use some binoculars** to try to find
a galaxy. Return to the area around
the Plough and look for a pair of tiny fuzzy
patches (shown here by two brown ovals).
These are galaxies. The brighter one is
a beautiful spiral galaxy called M81.

Southern star-hopping

Stargazers who live in the Southern Hemisphere don't have the advantage of a pole star to help them hop around the night sky. But, they can see far more bright stars in the polar region, as well as colourful nebulas, galaxies, and star-packed parts of our own galaxy – the Milky Way. Crux and the Southern Pointers are the starting points for a hop around the southern sky.

1 **First, locate the Southern Cross** and Southern Pointers (Alpha and Beta Centauri). Draw a line **(a)** from Beta Centauri through the bottom of the Southern Cross and extend it by the same distance again. You'll reach a red cloud in the constellation Carina – the Eta Carinae Nebula (shown as a red square). Take a closer look at this fabulous sight with binoculars. Deep inside is a massive star (Eta Carinae) that is likely to explode in the distant future.

2 **Close to the nebula** are two beautiful star clusters – NGC 3532 (shown as orange dots) and the Southern Pleiades. Through binoculars they look like sparkling jewels. Look at the Southern Pleiades without binoculars and count the stars. You'll find you can count more stars when you look slightly to one side of it.

Polar constellations

Southern Cross (Crux) ▶

The Southern Cross is in the main band of the Milky Way. Near its base is a dark patch in the Milky Way – a dust cloud called the Coalsack. The foot of the Cross is the star Acrux (in fact, a double star). The top is a red giant called Gamma Crucis.

◀ Centaurus

The Southern Pointers are part of the constellation Centaurus, which is said to resemble the mythical beast called a centaur, a creature half-man and half-horse. Alpha Centauri is the third-brightest star in the sky and the nearest star that's visible to the naked eye, at only 4.4 light-years away from Earth.

Carina ▶

The constellation Carina contains the brightest nebula in the night sky (the Eta Carinae Nebula). From the Greek for the "keel" of a boat, Carina stretches across to brilliant Canopus, the second-brightest star in the sky. Canopus is 15,000 times brighter than the Sun, but is so far away it doesn't blind us.

◀ Hydrus

The faint constellation Hydrus – which means water snake – is very close to the Small Magellanic Cloud. Like many southern constellations, Hydrus was named relatively recently by European explorers when they sailed the southern seas. With good binoculars, you can see a pair of red giant stars in the middle of Hydrus.

Triangulum Australe ▶

The three bright stars of Triangulum Australe stand out strongly against the hazy background of the Milky Way, in which this constellation lies. Triangulum Australe – or Southern Triangle – was named by European explorers in the sixteenth century. Sweep the area around it with binoculars to see if you can find the star cluster NGC 6025.

HYDRUS

Small Magellanic Cloud

47 Tucanae

3 **Now, draw a line (b)** from the top of the Southern Cross, past the Eta Carinae nebula, and onwards by the same distance again. This takes you to what looks like another cross – the "false cross", which often confuses stargazers. Just beyond it is star cluster IC 2391 that's worthy of closer inspection with binoculars.

4 **Draw the next line (c)** continuing the long bar of the Southern Cross straight out across the empty part of the sky to a small, fuzzy cloud – the Small Magellanic Cloud (see also page 67). This cloud is a small galaxy, 200,000 light-years from Earth. Through binoculars, you can see nebulas and star clusters within it. Close by is the second-best globular cluster (a dense ball of very ancient stars) in the night sky, called 47 Tucanae.

5 **Finally, return** to the Southern Pointers and draw a line **(d)** from Alpha Centauri to discover three bright stars in a triangle shape. This is the constellation Triangulum Australe.

The time at night

Whether you live in the Southern or the Northern Hemisphere, you can use the stars to tell the time. Make this star clock and learn how to use it, to the amazement of your friends. You'll need to know how to find the celestial pole (see pages 48–49).

The Plough

WHAT YOU WILL NEED

- Access to a photocopier or scanner and printer
- Paper or card
- Glue
- Scissors
- Paper fastener

Northern Hemisphere – base disc

Using your clock

Hold the star clock vertically in front of you. Turn it so that the date is at the top. Keep the base disc still and turn the top disc on the front until the constellations match their positions in the sky. Read off the time from the small hole.

The Plough

1 **If you live** in the Northern Hemisphere, use the two discs on this page. If you live in the Southern Hemisphere, use the two discs on the right. Photocopy them on to stiff paper or photocopy them on to ordinary paper and glue the larger disc to a circle of card to keep it stiff. Alternatively, scan them into a computer and print off on stiff paper.

TIME

Cassiopeia

Pole Star

The Plough

Instructions
Face due north, using the Pole Star to work out where north is. Hold the star clock vertically in front of you. Turn it so that the date is at the top. Keep the base disc still and turn the top disc on the front until the constellations match their position in the sky. Read off the time from the small hole.

Northern Hemisphere – top disc

TWENTY-FOUR HOURS

The 24-hour clock can be traced back to ancient Egyptian stargazers. From paintings on coffins up to 4,000 years old, we know they used the sky as a clock. They watched for certain stars to rise at intervals through the night. On average, 12 of their chosen stars came up between sunset and sunrise, so they divided the night into 12 periods. About 2,000 years ago, the Greek astronomer Hipparchus first suggested dividing a whole day and night into 24 equal hours.

▲ **Clock watching**
Ancient Egyptians watching the clock stars using an alignment device called a "merkhet".

Turn the top disc but keep the bottom disc still

Southern Hemisphere – base disc

Instructions
Face due south, using the Southern Cross and Southern Pointers to work out where the south celestial pole is. Hold the star clock vertically in front of you. Turn it so that the date is at the top. Keep the base disc still and turn the top disc on the front until the constellations match their position in the sky. Read off the time from the small hole.

Southern Hemisphere – top disc

2 **Carefully cut out** the two discs. Place the smaller disc on the centre of the large disc, punch a hole through the centre of both, and fix them together with a paper fastener.

Latitude locator

Before the days of satellites and accurate maps, sailors and explorers used the stars to find their way. The stars not only told them which way was north, but also the latitude – how far they were from Earth's equator. The device they used to work out their latitude was a quadrant, a simple viewing device that you can make yourself. As well as using a quadrant to work out your latitude, you can use it to measure the angle (altitude) of stars and planets above the horizon.

WHAT YOU WILL NEED

- Compasses
- Card
- Pen
- Protractor
- Scissors
- Paper
- Adhesive tape
- String
- Large heavy washer or similar weight

LOCATION LOCATION LOCATION

You can specify your location anywhere on Earth with two numbers: longitude and latitude. Longitude divides the world into 360 sections from pole to pole, like segments of an orange. Lines of latitude run east to west and show you how far you are from the equator. To understand latitude, imagine standing on the North Pole, where the Pole Star is always overhead. If you point at it, your arm will be at 90° to the ground – the North Pole's latitude is 90°. Now, imagine you're at the equator. The Pole Star is on the horizon, so your outstretched arm makes an angle of 0°.

Lines of longitude and latitude

Pierce hole here for string

Degrees of latitude

30° 40 50° 60° 70° 80° 90°

Using your quadrant
If you live in the Northern Hemisphere, find the Pole Star (see page 48). Look through the tube at the Pole Star, let the weight settle, then grip it. Look where the string falls to read off your latitude. If you live in the Southern Hemisphere, finding latitude is easiest when the Southern Cross (see page 49) is upright or upside-down. Look through the tube at Acrux, the base of the Southern Cross. If the Cross is upright, subtract 27° from your quadrant's reading; if it is upside-down, add 27°.

HANDY TIP

If you can, rest your elbow on a surface to steady both your view and the weight.

Roll stiff paper around a pen and tape closed

1 **Draw a quarter circle** on stiff card, cut it out, and use a protractor to mark a scale of degrees around the curved edge – running from 0° to 90°. Leave a border of about 1 cm (½ in) either side of the scale (don't put 0° and 90° right at the edges).

2 **Make a hole** in the corner, taking care to align it perfectly to both the 0° and the 90° gradations. Tie a piece of string, which is attached to a weight, through the hole.

3 **Make the viewing tube** by rolling a piece of paper around a pen. Tape the tube to the 90° side of the quadrant, taking care to make it perfectly straight.

A star is born

New stars are born inside vast gas clouds called nebulas, which lie between the stars. One of the most spectacular nebulas you can see is the Orion Nebula, which is visible from the Northern and the Southern Hemispheres.

1 **The best time to see** the Orion Nebula, which is in the constellation of Orion, is from December to February, when it's high in the night sky. If you live in the Northern Hemisphere, look south. If you live in the Southern Hemisphere, look north.

The Orion constellation

Horsehead Nebula

Alnitak

Orion Nebula

2 **When you've spotted** the distinctive shape of Orion, look for the three stars that make up Orion's "belt". Hanging from the belt is Orion's "sword", in the middle of which is the Orion Nebula. You can see the nebula with the naked eye, but binoculars will reveal more detail. Deep inside this cloud, new stars are forming. Photographs of the Orion Nebula reveal glorious colours. Unfortunately, you can't see these colours with the naked eye or binoculars.

3 **Look again at the star** in the centre of the Orion Nebula. With the naked eye you can see one star, but with binoculars you might see two. In fact, there's a group of at least four newly formed stars called the Trapezium, after their shape, right in the heart of the nebula. The energy emitted by these new stars is making the gas in the nebula glow.

Orion the Hunter

Orion is named after a hunter in Greek myths. Southern Hemisphere viewers see the hunter upside-down, with his feet at the top and shoulders at the bottom.

Horsehead Nebula

4 **If you had** a powerful telescope, you could search for another interesting nebula in Orion, shown in the picture above. It's called the Horsehead Nebula, because of its shape. It is actually a dark cloud of dust silhouetted against the red gas cloud behind it. The Horsehead Nebula is just below Alnitak, the left star in Orion's belt.

Starbirth nebulas

Stars form when the force of gravity makes pockets of gas in nebulas shrink. Exactly the same process gave birth to our Sun (see page 11). The gas in most starbirth nebulas is too faint to see, even with binoculars. However, cameras can capture the hazy colours with breathtaking results.

North America Nebula ▶
This curious nebula in the constellation Cygnus looks like a map of North America, complete with its own Gulf of Mexico. The nebula is lit up by the newly formed stars within it.

Lagoon Nebula ▶
The Lagoon Nebula is in the constellation Sagittarius and is easy to see with the naked eye, or via binoculars. This close-up image from the Hubble Space Telescope shows twisted columns of gas and a new star.

Trifid Nebula ▶
This nebula is also in Sagittarius. You can just see it with binoculars, but you need a good telescope to see any level of detail. The dark bands crossing the nebula are lanes of dust that block the light.

Columns in the Eagle Nebula ▶
These colossal pillars of hydrogen gas were also photographed by the Hubble Space Telescope. New stars are forming in the "fingers" of gas at the top of the biggest pillar. The fingers are bigger than our solar system.

Find the Seven Sisters

The Seven Sisters is the common name for a star cluster called the Pleiades. Oddly, nobody actually sees seven stars in the Pleiades – most people see six. Good eyesight, or binoculars, actually reveals more than seven.

When to look

If you live in the Northern Hemisphere, the best time to see the Pleiades is in autumn or winter. For southerners, the best views are in spring and summer. The cluster reaches its highest point in the sky at midnight in November. The image (right) is a highly magnified view.

WHAT YOU WILL NEED

- No equipment essential, but binoculars and a planisphere are useful

1 **First, locate** Orion and its belt. (To find out more about Orion, look on pages 58–59). In the Northern Hemisphere, you should draw an imaginary line **(a)** up through Orion's belt, past the shoulder of Orion, and onwards to a bright, reddish star called Aldebaran, which is part of the constellation Taurus. If you live in the Southern Hemisphere, where Orion is upside-down, draw the line down from his belt and then on to Aldebaran.

2 **If you have binoculars,** take a close look at Aldebaran, a red giant star that varies slightly in brightness. (Find out about red giants on pages 62–63.) Next to Aldebaran, you can see an open star cluster (see box right) called the Hyades.

3 **Now, hop beyond** Aldebaran, travelling away from Orion in roughly the same direction but for a slightly shorter distance **(b)**. You'll come to the Pleiades star cluster – one of the most beautiful sights in the night sky.

The starlight from the Pleiades takes about 400 years to reach Earth

STAR CLUSTERS

Double star cluster in LMC NGC 1850

Tightly packed groups of stars are called star clusters and there are two main types. Open clusters, such as the Hyades and the Pleiades, are loose groups of young, hot stars that glow with a bluish brilliance. Globular clusters, on the other hand, are dense balls of hundreds of thousands of very ancient stars. Unlike open clusters, which lie within the Milky Way galaxy, globular clusters are often above or below the galaxy's plane. One of the most spectacular is Omega Centauri in the constellation Centaurus, which is visible from the Southern Hemisphere. The most impressive globular cluster visible to northern viewers is the Hercules Cluster, in the Hercules constellation.

4 **Take a good look** at the Pleiades with the naked eye. How many stars can you count? If you have binoculars, look again. Can you count more? There are actually more than 3,000 stars in the Pleiades. At only 78 million years old, these stars are babies in astronomical terms, and wouldn't have been in the night sky during the age of the dinosaurs. With a powerful telescope you can see a blue haze around the stars, which is a dust cloud through which the stars are currently passing.

Going, going, gone

All stars eventually run out of energy and die. As they grow older, their surface cools down and turns red. Stars also swell in size with age, becoming "red giants" and "red supergiants". Such stars are easy to spot, and their warm colour is obvious even to the naked eye.

If Betelgeuse blew up

Betelgeuse is a red supergiant in Orion. Astronomers think it's near the end of its life and is about to blow apart, in a colossal explosion called a supernova. The artist's impression on the right shows what a Betelgeuse supernova might look like from Earth. For a few weeks, the star would outshine the Moon and cast shadows on Earth.

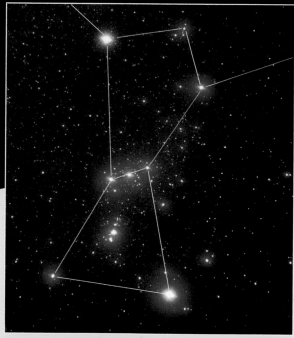

The Orion constellation

1 **One of the easiest** red supergiants to see is Betelgeuse, on the left shoulder of Orion (as we look at it). Betelgeuse is about 800 times wider than our Sun. Look at Betelgeuse with binoculars, and compare its colour to the blue supergiant Rigel – the very bright star in the opposite corner of Orion (the right foot). Blue supergiants form when red supergiants lose some of their outer atmosphere. They can also explode as supernovas.

Red stars
3,000°C
(5,400°F)

Orange stars
4,000°C
(7,200°F)

Yellow stars
6,000°C
(10,800°F)

White stars
10,000°C
(18,000°F)

Light-blue stars
20,000°C
(36,000°F)

Blue stars
50,000°C
(90,000°F)

2 **You can tell** a star's surface temperature from its colour. Blue stars are the hottest, red are the coolest. Use the guide above to work out the temperature of these stars: Rigel, Vega (the brightest star in Lyra), Arcturus (brightest star in Boötes), Capella (brightest star in Auriga), Sirius (brightest star in Canis Major), and Deneb (brightest star in Cygnus).

WHEN STARS DIE

What happens when a star dies depends on its weight. Light stars swell into red giants and then throw off their outer layers into space, forming ghostly clouds called planetary nebulas, leaving behind a small star called a white dwarf. Massive stars swell into much bigger red supergiants. When they finally run out of enough energy to resist the awesome inward pull of their own gravity, they collapse in an instant. The collapse creates a devastating shock wave that hurls out the star's outer layers in an explosion brighter than a billion suns, called a supernova. The dense core may then survive as a "neutron star". But, the most massive cores continue to shrink under their gravity until they are smaller than an atom. The result is a black hole – a gravitational trap from which nothing can escape.

Black holes ▲
This artist's impression shows a black hole (left) sucking in a spinning cloud of matter from a neighbouring blue giant star (right).

Awesome Antares
If you live in the Southern Hemisphere, look for the red supergiant Antares, the brightest star in Scorpius. Antares is one of the reddest stars in the sky. It's almost as bright as Betelgeuse and about 1 billion km (620 million miles) wide, making it 700 times wider than the Sun.

The red supergiant Antares (far left)

Our local galaxy

Almost every star you can see in the night sky belongs to the Milky Way – our local galaxy. The Milky Way is a gargantuan, spinning whirlpool of 200 billion stars, most of which are clustered in the centre, or spread along spiral arms. On dark, clear nights, you can sometimes see it stretching across the sky as a hazy band.

Spiral arms curve out from the heart of galaxy NGC 1232

Distorting dust

Dust clouds in some parts of the Milky Way block out the light from the stars beyond, creating dark lanes in our view of the galaxy. In the picture above, dark clouds of dust have mixed with glowing gas clouds, creating a multicoloured spectacle.

From a distance

If you could see the Milky Way from a great distance, it might look like the spiral galaxy NGC 1232. Because we're inside the Milky Way, we see it side-on and can't see its spiral shape. If there were no dust clouds in the way, we might get a view like the one below. This image shows the galaxy's flat shape and central bulge, where stars are packed most densely. From side to side, the whole Milky Way measures about 1 billion billion km (600 million billion miles).

Galaxy NGC 1232

Our solar system is in one of the spiral arms about halfway from the centre

The Milky Way viewed side-on from space

Viewing the Milky Way

To see the Milky Way in all its glory,
you need a clear, moonless night, free of light
pollution. Parts of the Milky Way are visible for
much of the year, but to see the best areas you need
to know when and where to look. Northern Hemisphere
viewers should look at the constellations Cygnus and
Aquila in late summer. In the Southern Hemisphere,
you should look at Sagittarius and Scorpius in winter
for a stunning view of the galaxy's star-packed centre.

GALAXY IN A CUP

You can make a model of the Milky Way with
everyday ingredients, such as coffee and cream.
Ask an adult to make a cup of black coffee for you.
Stir the coffee quite quickly to make it spin, then
gently lower in a spoonful of cream. The cream
will form a spinning spiral. In reality, the Milky
Way spins in a very different way from cream in a
coffee cup. The spiral arms don't rotate as whole
objects – they are simply places where stars get
temporarily crowded during their journey around
the galaxy, like cars passing through a traffic jam.

A home-made spiral galaxy

Galaxy hunting

If you know where to look, you can see far beyond our local galaxy. Spot three of the Milky Way's closest neighbours, including its two satellite galaxies, and the most distant object visible to the human eye.

Andromeda galaxy
The Andromeda galaxy is the most distant object the naked eye can see. It's about 2.5 million light-years away, which means we see it as it was 2.5 million years ago, before humans had even evolved. It's a spiral galaxy, like the Milky Way, but one-and-a-half times the size, with 400 billion stars. Near it are two small companion galaxies, one of which (M32) is visible in this picture as a fuzzy white spot.

M32

CASSIOPEIA

a

Andromeda galaxy

c

b PEGASUS

Algenib

On good nights you might see ten stars in the Great Square of Pegasus; on poor nights it appears empty

1 **In the Northern Hemisphere,** Andromeda is the easiest galaxy to see. To star-hop to it, start with the "W"-shaped constellation Cassiopeia (see pages 50–51). Draw a line **(a)** from the middle star in Cassiopeia, through the star at the deepest point in the W, and on to a bright star at the corner of a large square. The square is part of the constellation Pegasus, which is named after a mythological winged horse.

2 **Now, hop anticlockwise (b)** around the Great Square of Pegasus to the next star, Algenib. Draw a line **(c)** from Algenib back up to Cassiopeia. Just past halfway along is a blurry oval – the Andromeda galaxy. The galaxy is visible to the naked eye in good conditions, and binoculars will reveal the galaxy's bright centre. With a big telescope, the spiral arms are visible too. With good binoculars you might just be able to see one of the Andromeda galaxy's small companion galaxies, known as M32.

Large Magellanic Cloud

This galaxy is one of our closest neighbours, 170,000 light-years away. It orbits the Milky Way as a satellite and is only a fraction of the size of the Milky Way. The Large and Small Magellanic Clouds are named after the Portuguese explorer, Ferdinand Magellan, who saw them on the first round-the-world sailing trip.

WHAT YOU WILL NEED

- No equipment essential, but binoculars and a planisphere are useful

1 **In the Southern Hemisphere**, the easiest galaxies to see are the Large and the Small Magellanic Clouds. From the far south, these can be seen in the sky all year round. To locate the Large Magellanic Cloud, start from the Southern Cross. Draw a line **(a)** from Beta Crucis through Acrux, and extend it until you reach a cloudy patch – this is the Large Magellanic Cloud. Using binoculars, you might be able to see star clusters and nebulas within this galaxy. The largest nebula is the Tarantula Nebula.

2 **To find the** Small Magellanic Cloud, draw a line **(b)** down the long shaft of the Southern Cross and extend it to another cloudy patch near the Hydrus constellation. Binoculars may help to reveal star clusters and nebulas within it.

Expanding universe

The universe is everything – planets, stars, galaxies, and all the nothingness in between. Astronomers have discovered that the universe is getting bigger, but could it carry on growing forever? It is difficult for the mind to picture, but this simple activity with a balloon can help you to understand this expansion.

Ballooning out

The universe isn't expanding "into" anything because there's no space outside it and no outer edge. Imagine the galaxies are on the surface of a balloon. Like the universe, the balloon's surface has no centre and no outer boundary, yet it can still expand.

THE ACCELERATING UNIVERSE

Hubble Space Telescope image of remote galaxies and stars

When astronomers point their most powerful telescopes at tiny areas of the sky, they get pictures like the one above. It shows galaxies stretching into the distance as far as we can see, each one home to billions of stars and planets. Careful observations show that all the galaxies are getting further apart, so the whole universe must be expanding. Oddly, the expansion is speeding up, yet the force of gravity ought to slow it down. Astronomers think the universe must therefore be full of an invisible force called "dark energy" that is somehow repelling gravity and pushing everything apart. The same force may have played a role in the Big Bang.

WHAT YOU WILL NEED

• Balloons
• Permanent marker pen

1 **Use a permanent** marker pen to draw galaxies on a balloon. If you find it easier, you can do this after you have first inflated it a little.

THE BIG BANG

When the universe began

The universe began 13.7 billion years ago, when it exploded out of nothingness. In a second, it grew from being tinier than an atom to 200 million billion km (125 million billion miles) wide. It has been expanding ever since and may do so forever. Some scientists think time itself began in the Big Bang – that may always remain a mystery.

Draw spirals to represent galaxies

2 **Blow up the balloon** and tie the end. The galaxies have become much larger and spread further apart. The galaxies in the real universe are also getting further apart, but they're not growing in size.

The galaxies move apart as the balloon expands

Glossary

Asteroid A rocky body in the solar system that can be as big as 1,000 km (620 miles) wide. Most asteroids lie in a belt between Mars and Jupiter.

Astronomy The scientific study of space.

Atmosphere The layer of gas trapped around a planet by the force of gravity.

Atom The smallest unit of matter, which cannot be divided into smaller parts, except in a nuclear reaction.

Axis An imaginary line that passes through the centre of a planet, or other body, and around which the body rotates.

Big Bang The violent explosion that gave birth to the universe 13.7 billion years ago.

Billion A number equivalent to one thousand million.

Black hole A point in space with such a powerful gravitational pull that nothing, not even light, can escape.

Celestial pole The point at the top or bottom of the celestial sphere. The north and south celestial poles do not move during the night and are always due north or due south.

Celestial sphere An imaginary globe that surrounds Earth. Stars move around Earth as if fixed points on this sphere.

Circumpolar star A star that does not set, but remains above the horizon, and circles the celestial pole.

Comet A celestial body made of ice and rocky dust. When a comet nears the Sun, its surface evaporates and releases gas and dust in glowing tails.

Constellation A pattern of stars in the sky, often named after a mythological person or creature.

Core The innermost part of a star or planet.

Corona The faint upper atmosphere of the Sun, which is visible as a halo only during a total solar eclipse.

Cosmos An alternative name for the universe.

Crater A bowl-shaped depression formed by a meteorite impact or by a volcanic eruption.

Crust The outer, rocky part of a planet or moon.

Dark energy A theoretical force that is thought to be causing the accelerating expansion of the universe. Its true nature is a mystery.

Degree A unit used in measuring angles or distances across a sphere or globe.

Dwarf planet A celestial body orbiting the Sun, but not a planet or a moon.

Eclipse The effect when the shadow of a moon, or planet, is cast on another celestial body.

Ecliptic The imaginary line around the sky that traces the movement of the Sun through the year.

Ellipse An oval shape. The orbits of planets are ellipses.

Escape velocity The speed at which an object must travel to escape the pull of gravity.

Galaxy A group of millions or billions of stars held together by gravity.

Giant planet A large planet that is made mainly of hydrogen. Giant planets are sometimes called gas giants, though they consist mostly of liquid rather than gas. Jupiter, Saturn, Uranus, and Neptune are giant planets.

Globular cluster A dense ball of very ancient stars.

Gravity The invisible force of attraction that exists between all objects.

Greenhouse effect The process by which heat radiated from the ground is trapped by gases in the atmosphere, such as carbon dioxide, leading to global warming.

Hydrogen The most common chemical element in the universe. Hydrogen is the main component of stars and galaxies.

Interstellar A term that means "between the stars".

Latitude A measure of the distance north or south of Earth's equator. Latitude is measured in degrees and shown on globes as lines parallel to the equator.

Light pollution The glow in the sky caused by street lights and atmospheric pollution. Light pollution makes stargazing difficult in cities.

Light-year The unit of astronomical distance based on the distance light travels in a year – 10 million million km (6 million million miles).

Longitude A measure in degrees of the distance, east or west, from a line of 0°, which passes through Greenwich in London, England.

Magnitude The brightness of a star. Bright objects have low or negative numbers; faint objects have high numbers.

Mass A measure of the amount of matter in an object. Mass has a similar meaning to weight, but objects have weight only when they are on Earth or another large body with significant gravity.

Matter Any material that has mass and occupies space.

Meteor A rock that burns up as it enters Earth's atmosphere, forming a shooting star.

Meteor shower A period when the rate of shooting stars rises as Earth passes through the trail of dust left by a comet.

Meteorite A rock from space that falls to Earth's surface without burning up completely.

Milky Way The galaxy in which we live. It can be seen as a pale, milky band across the sky on dark nights.

Moon A large, natural object that orbits a planet.

Naked eye Human vision that is not enhanced in any way.

Nebula A vast cloud of gas and/or dust in space.

Nuclear fusion The joining of the nuclei of atoms. This process releases vast amounts of energy. Nuclear fusion is the energy source of stars.

Observatory A place where astronomers observe the night sky, often with a telescope.

Open cluster A loose cluster of young stars.

Opposition The point in the orbit of a planet when it is on the opposite side of Earth from the Sun, making viewing easy.

Orbit The path in which one object travels around another, more massive, object.

Planet A large, spherical body that orbits a star.

Planetary nebula A cloud of gas and dust puffed out by a dying star.

Planisphere A star chart with a rotating window that shows which stars are visible at particular times and dates, based on your latitude.

Pole Star The star Polaris that marks the north celestial pole, and around which the northern sky appears to rotate. The Pole Star is always due north.

Quadrillion A number equivalent to one thousand million million.

Red giant A star, near the end of its life, swollen and

reddened as it runs out of nuclear fuel.

Red supergiant A star that has reddened and swollen near the end of its life, before exploding in a supernova.

Rocky planet A type of planet made largely of rock. Mercury, Venus, Earth, and Mars are all rocky planets.

Satellite An object trapped in orbit around a planet. Moons are natural satellites.

Shooting star A meteor.

Solar system A sun and its surroundings, including planets and asteroids.

Star A gigantic globe of glowing gas, lit up by nuclear fusion reactions in its core.

Sunspot A relatively cool, dark spot on the Sun's surface.

Supernova A huge explosion that happens when a star dies.

Trillion A number equivalent to one million million.

Universe Everything that exists – planets, stars, galaxies, and all space in between.

Variable star A star that varies in brightness. Many variable stars also vary in size.

Void An immense empty region in space.

Zodiac The band of constellations along the ecliptic. Through the year, the Sun, Moon, and planets appear to move through the constellations of the zodiac.

Index

The author would like to thank Jon Woodcock for astronomical expertise.

Model Jack Williams

Index Hilary Bird

The publisher would like to thank the following for their kind permission to reproduce their photographs:
t = top, b = bottom, l = left, r = right, c = centre, a = above
Corbis/Gabe Palmer: 38–39c; NASA/Jet Propulsion Laboratory: 15tr, 20cl, 32bl, 32–33c, 35tr, 36–37, 37tr, b, 39 (Jupiter's moons), 40tl, 41tr; /Marshall Space Flight Center Art Collection: 28l; Science & Society Picture Library: 17tr, 54tr; Science Photo Library/ David Nunuk: 4–5, 18tr, 42–43 (background), 44–45 (background), /David A. Hardy: 8bl, 26bl, 63cr, 64b, / Detlev van Ravenswaay: 8–9t, 12, 19t, 56bl, 69tr, /

Frank Zullo: 9r, 42bl, 47tl, 64–65 (background), /John Foster: 11bl, /David Ducros: 13tr, 27r, /Mark Garlick: 14bl, 43tr, 68–69, /Cordelia Molloy: 18cl, /Dr Fred Espenak: 18–19b, 24–25t, /John Sanford: 20bl, 20–21 (night sky), 31cl, 56–57 (night sky), 58–59 (background), 62l, /Eckhard Slawik: 20–21 (moon), 23 (moon phases), 54–55 (night sky), /European Southern Observatory: 22tr, 59cl, 64c, /Larry Landolfi: 24bl, 38t, /Dr Juerg Alean: 25b, /NASA: 29tr, 30l, /Pekka Parviainen: 30–31t, 48–49 (background) /NASA/SMU/David P. Anderson: 31cr, /Space Telescope Science Institute/NASA: 33tr, 59cra, 59br, /Rev. Ronald Royer: 39bl, /Jerry Schad: 46–47 (background), /Tony & Daphne Hallas: 58l, 66–67 (background), /Celestial Image Company: 59tr, 61br, 67t, /National Optical Astronomy Observatories: 59crb, /Royal Observatory, Edinburgh: 60–61 (background), /Joe Tucciarone: 62–63 (background), /Luke Dodd: 63b, /MPIA-HD,

Birkle, Slawik: 64tl; STScI, Hubble Space Telescope: 5cr, 68b. Dorling Kindersley: NASA / JPL 75tl, 78tc, 79cla, The London Planetarium 74tl, 75tc, NASA 74tc, 74cl, 74c, 74cr, 75cla, 75br, 78crb; Dreamstime. com: Eraxion 79br, Andrej Kaprinay 5cra; ESO: 78cla, 78cra; Fotolia: Paul Paladin 75bl, Alexey Repka 78tr; Getty Images: Stocktrek Images 78c; NASA: ESA, Hubble Heritage 79cr, JPL 74cra, 78clb, 79crb, JPL-Caltech 74cb, 79clb, Marshall Space Flight Center Art Collection 79bl, MSFC 79tc, The Hubble Heritage Team, (STScI / AURA), ESA 75bc, 78ftl, X-ray: NASA / CXC / SAO; Optical: NASA / STScI; Infrared: NASA / JPL-Caltech 75tr, 75ca, 75cl.

All other images © Dorling Kindersley.

For further information see:
www.dkimages.com

Mercury

Venus

Earth

Mars

Jupiter

Orion constellation

Black hole

Red giant star

Skylab
space station

Galileo space probe

Milky Way

Pluto

Keck telescopes

Solar flare

Asteroid

Ganymede

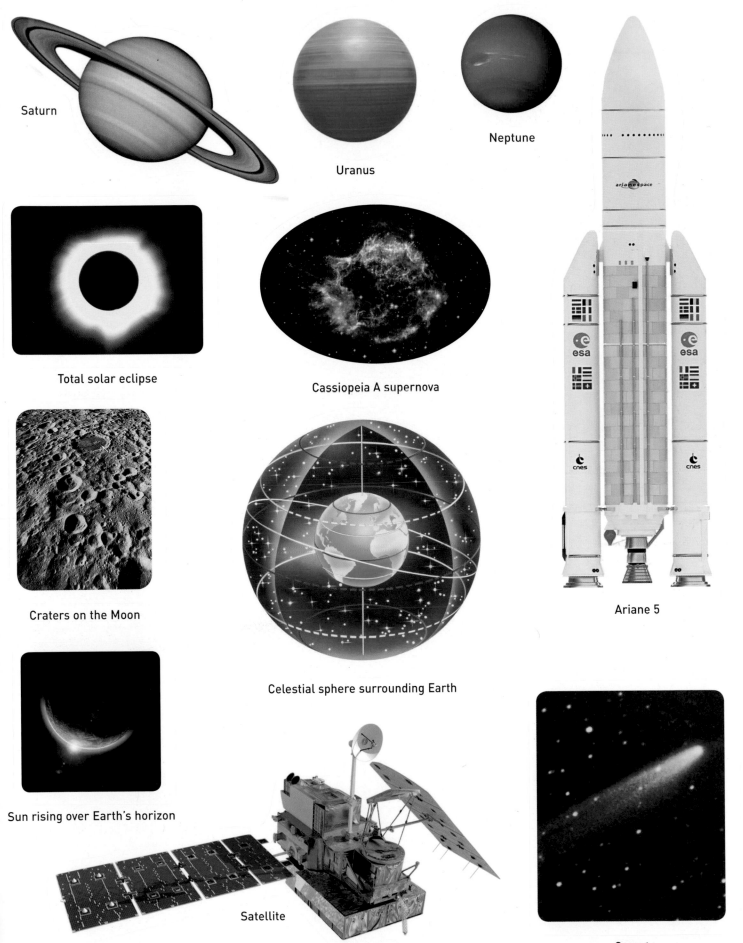

Saturn

Uranus

Neptune

Total solar eclipse

Cassiopeia A supernova

Craters on the Moon

Celestial sphere surrounding Earth

Ariane 5

Sun rising over Earth's horizon

Satellite

Comet

Eagle nebula

Europa

Cassiopeia

Full Moon

Star cluster NGC 3603

Crux

Voyager space probe

Horsehead nebula

North America nebula

Carina

Moon rock

Hydrus

Telescope

Cepheus

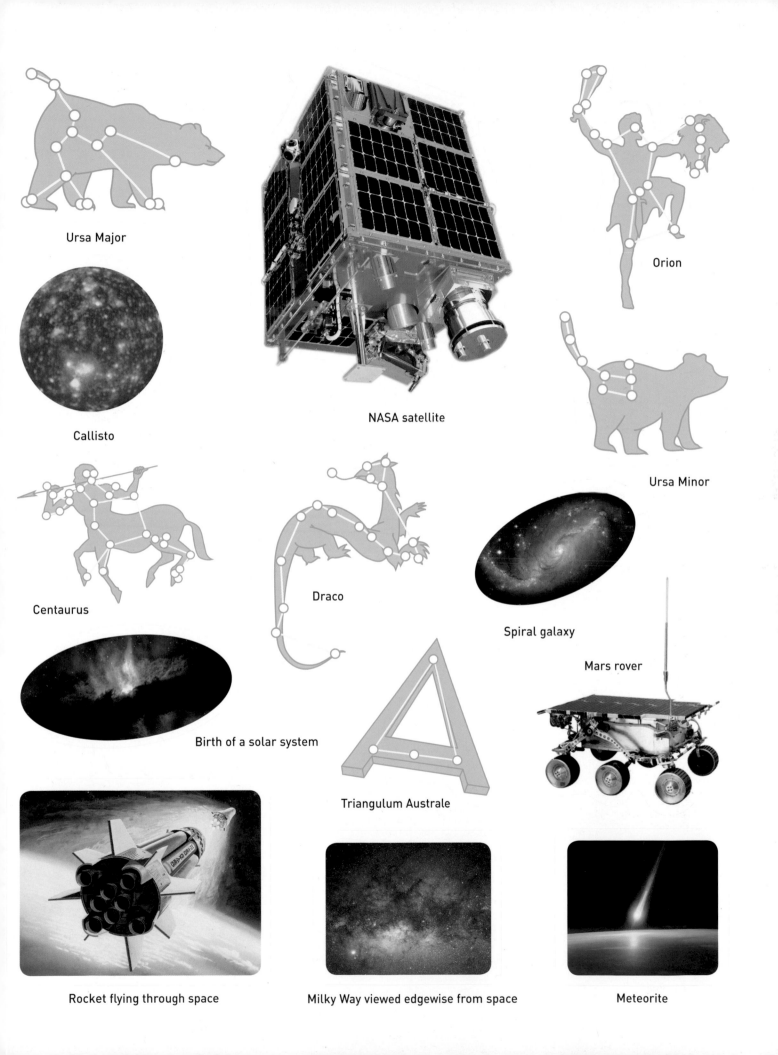

Ursa Major

Callisto

NASA satellite

Orion

Ursa Minor

Centaurus

Draco

Spiral galaxy

Mars rover

Birth of a solar system

Triangulum Australe

Rocket flying through space

Milky Way viewed edgewise from space

Meteorite